The Ninjabread Man

'The Ninjabread Man'
An original concept by Rebecca Colby
© Rebecca Colby 2022

Illustrated by Giusi Capizzi

Published by MAVERICK ARTS PUBLISHING LTD
Studio 11, City Business Centre, 6 Brighton Road,
Horsham, West Sussex, RH13 5BB
© Maverick Arts Publishing Limited February 2022
+44 (0)1403 256941

A CIP catalogue record for this book is available at the British Library.

ISBN 978-1-84886-854-0

www.maverickbooks.co.uk

This book is rated as: Orange Band (Guided Reading)
It follows the requirements for Phase 5 phonics.
Most words are decodable, and any non-decodable words are familiar,
supported by the context and/or represented in the artwork.

The Ninjabread Man

by Rebecca Colby

illustrated by
Giusi Capizzi

Once, there was a little, old man who wanted a friend.

He wanted a friend to garden with him and read with him...

...and do karate with him.

One day, the old man read a story and had an idea.

He went to the kitchen and baked

a Gingerbread Man.

While he waited for the Gingerbread Man to cook, he fell asleep.

When the old man woke up,

the Gingerbread Man was burnt.

It was a Ninjabread Man!

The Ninjabread Man made a cloud of
icing sugar, and ran away.

The old man put on his glasses.

He didn't see the Ninjabread Man

until it was too late.

The Ninjabread Man ran into a wood.

He came to a tea house.

No one will catch me here.

A lady was inside the tea house.

Everything was ready for tea.

"Come in!" said the lady. "You are just in time for my tea!" She licked her lips. The Ninjabread Man threw one of his stars and ran away.

The Ninjabread Man ran and ran
until he came to a school.

"It looks safe here," he said.

But there was nowhere to hide
in the school.

The Ninjabread Man tossed his rope and swung across the room.

Fight, fight, as hard as you can. You can't catch me, I'm the Ninjabread Man.

The students tried to catch the Ninjabread Man, but he ran away.

He saw one more place to hide.

"No one will catch me here!"

It was dark inside.

The Ninjabread Man couldn't see a thing.

"Hello?" he said. Something creaked.

"Is anyone there?"

Something
crunched.

"Who is it?"

Something

snapped.

Then he saw white circles.

They were eyes. Lots of eyes!

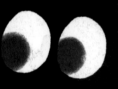

Run, run, as fast as you can!

We'll still get you...

Quiz

1. What happened while the Gingerbread Man was cooking?
a) The old man did karate
b) The oven turned off
c) The old man fell asleep

2. What did the Ninjabread Man make a cloud out of?
a) Icing sugar
b) Flour
c) Chocolate sprinkles

3. What did the Ninjabread Man throw at the lady?
a) A star
b) A circle
c) A triangle

4. How did the Ninjabread Man swing across the room at school?
a) With his stars
b) With his rope
c) With his icing

5. At the end, what group was the Ninjabread Man invited to join?
a) A karate club
b) A cooking class
c) A ninja clan

Turn over for answers

Book Bands for Guided Reading

The Institute of Education book banding system is a scale of colours that reflects the various levels of reading difficulty. The bands are assigned by taking into account the content, the language style, the layout and phonics. Word, phrase and sentence level work is also taken into consideration.

Maverick Early Readers are a bright, attractive range of books covering the pink to white bands. All of these books have been book banded for guided reading to the industry standard and edited by a leading educational consultant.

Pink
Red
Yellow
Blue
Green
Orange
Turquoise
Purple
Gold
White

To view the whole Maverick Readers scheme, visit our website at
www.maverickearlyreaders.com

Or scan the QR code above to view our scheme instantly!

Quiz Answers: 1c, 2a, 3a, 4b, 5c